# A Needle in Her Cloth

## The Red Plaid Dress Collection

Sherree Dawn Gray Sanders

This is a work of fiction. All of the characters, names, incidents, organizations, and dialogue in this novel are either the products of the author's imagination or are used fictitiously.

Scripture quotations are from the ESV® Bible (The Holy Bible, English Standard Version®), copyright © 2001 by Crossway, a publishing ministry of Good News Publishers. Used by permission. All rights reserved.

Scripture quotations marked (NLT) are taken from the Holy Bible, New Living Translation, copyright ©1996, 2004, 2015 by Tyndale House Foundation. Used by permission of Tyndale House Publishers, Inc., Carol Stream, Illinois 60188. All rights reserved.

Scripture quotations marked (NIV) are taken from the Holy Bible, New International Version®, NIV®. Copyright © 1973, 1978, 1984, 2011 by Biblica, Inc.™ Used by permission of Zondervan. All rights reserved worldwide. www.zondervan.com The "NIV" and "New International Version" are trademarks registered in the United States Patent and Trademark Office by Biblica, Inc.™

WestBow Press books may be ordered through booksellers or by contacting:

WestBow Press
A Division of Thomas Nelson & Zondervan
1663 Liberty Drive
Bloomington, IN 47403
www.westbowpress.com
1 (866) 928-1240

Because of the dynamic nature of the Internet, any web addresses or links contained in this book may have changed since publication and may no longer be valid. The views expressed in this work are solely those of the author and do not necessarily reflect the views of the publisher, and the publisher hereby disclaims any responsibility for them.

Any people depicted in stock imagery provided by Getty Images are models, and such images are being used for illustrative purposes only. Certain stock imagery © Getty Images.

ISBN: 978-1-9736-5468-1 (sc)
ISBN: 978-1-9736-6094-1 (hc)
ISBN: 978-1-9736-5469-8 (e)

Library of Congress Control Number: 2019902159

Print information available on the last page.

WestBow Press rev. date: 6/25/2019

WestBow
PRESS®
A DIVISION OF THOMAS NELSON
& ZONDERVAN

Our life's statement begins with the day we are born and ends with one last breath. What we create during this time is our life's story, and it is written with the choices we make.

\* To Kristina \*

# Acknowledgements

First, I would like to thank my readers who bring my inspiration full circle. Without you, none of this would be possible. I would also like to thank Mitchell's Photography and my publisher, Westbow Press, Inc., for their diligent support in this endeavor. But most of all, I am thankful to my daughter, Kristina, for her initial and continued encouragement of this book.

"The Lord is merciful and compassionate...
filled with unfailing love."

Psalm 145:8 NLT

# Red Plaid Dress

I want to paint a picture
    of my youth in '65,
Carolina country farms
    where neighbors were so kind.
I recall a red plaid dress
    with crisp lace around the collar
Blowing in the wind
    on a porch in Colfax holler.
The sun was setting brightly
    in the oaks of the western sky;
The Chatterbox was a fruit stand
    that we did oft pass by.
I didn't have any dresses
    for school, which was starting soon;
We didn't have much money
    but just enough to do.
Mom and Dad worked 8 to 5 –
    we didn't have much then,
But we had more than some of the folks
    way back when.
Red plaid dress with crisp white collar
    blowing in the breeze in Colfax holler.
Living in the country making little dresses;
    "Cars pass by. They'll buy them, I'm guessin'."

Light blue Chevy pick-up truck
    easing down a country road.
Dad says, "Let's stop a minute
    before we go on home."
A lean-to fruit stand
    with a gravel driveway,
Tires rolling in the rocks,
    I can still hear them today.
"Let's help this guy out, Honey."
"You like apples, don't you, Sherry?"
"We'll take this bag of apples
    that look so very fine."
"Thank you so much, Sir. You know,
    I can't spare a dime."
One-room house with peeling paint
    beside the Chatterbox,

Tired woman on the steps
     with a needle in her cloth,
And hanging from a wire
     stretched across the porch in shade,
Were plaid little girl dresses
     that the man's wife had made.
Red plaid dress with crisp white collar
     blowing in the breeze in Colfax holler.
Living in the country making little dresses;
     "Cars pass by. They'll buy them, I'm guessin'."
Puffy short-sleeved dresses
     that buttoned up the back,
With a yard of cotton gathered skirt
     and big wide bow sash.
Always dark plaid with little white collars
     blowing in the breeze in Colfax holler.

Mom said, "I like your dresses
    of plaid and collared lace."
"They would look so very pretty
    on her Shirley Temple face."
"I'll take those two dresses,
    and how much will that be?"
"I stitched them both with love
    and they are each only three."
And the woman in drab dress
    with daughter at her knee
Took the money, and I thought
    how that girl could be me.
I was witness to the pain
    in the woman's weathered eyes,
Which suddenly lifted up
    like the sun in the morning sky.
Red plaid dress with crisp white collar
    blowing in the breeze in Colfax holler.
Living in the country making little dresses;
    "Cars pass by. They'll buy them, I'm guessin'."
School girls made fun
    of my dresses with white collars.
Laughing, "Where did you get them?
    The fruit stand in the holler?"
Dad said they were poor
    and couldn't spare a dime,
So I wore those homemade dresses
    with an extra ounce of pride.
"If you look up 'rich man'
    in the Book of Jesus' name,

You will find we are all rich;
  by salvation we are claimed."
No pink or blue or green,
  no flowers or paisley print,
Just different plaids of dark red
  and that was it.
I didn't like the dresses
  but didn't fuss, cry or whine –
I wasn't old enough
  to understand at the time.
Now, I can have any dress that I desire
  from the best designers around –
But none can come close to competing
  with the dress made in my hometown.
Yes, I don't have to wear it ever again.
And today is a blessing from way back when.
Sewn with grace and love,
  I never knew the woman's name,
But the blessings I received from her
  were blessings just the same.
Red plaid dress with crisp white collar
  blowing in the breeze in Colfax holler.
Life was a little more bitter, unsweet
  than where I live now on Easy Girl Street.
And so as I grew older
  and passed by the house of dresses,
My heart would feel the touch
  of her butterfly caresses.
Red plaid dresses with lacy little collars,
Now I dance in gala gowns

worth hundreds of dollars.
But none have ever made me
more proud or content
Than the little red dresses
blowing in the wind.
Red plaid dress with crisp white collar
blowing in the breeze in Colfax holler…

Then Jesus said, "Come to me, all of you who are weary and carry heavy burdens, and I will give you rest."

Matthew 11:28 NLT

# Your Quiet Place

Everyone needs a special place
    where they can go and just "be" –
Alone with their thoughts, uninterrupted,
    and sit quietly.

We will call it a niche,
    a place with your name,
Where your heart is welcomed
    each day the very same.

There is no pretending
    in this friendship place.
Everything is okay
    in your sacred space.

You may see sunlight
    stream in from the door
And cast patterns of lace
    onto the floor.

Prisms of rainbows
    from beveled cut glass
May decorate the room
    as you think of the past.

Your corner may be dark,
    with ne'er a light be,
As you are comforted in the darkness
    where no one can see.

You may sit in sunshine
        on a wooden park bench,
Children playing all around,
        their joy for you to drench.

Maybe it's your favorite corner
        in a bedroom space,
Where you can sip your coffee or tea,
        taking life at your own pace.

It matters not the location
        of your very special place,
Just that you and God have a spot:
        your own quiet place.

"Every good and perfect gift is from above, coming down from the Father of the heavenly lights, who does not change like shifting shadows."

James 1:17 NIV

# The Only Sunflower

The girl worked in the garden
>with July sun beaming down;

She wiped the beads of salty sweat
>from her forehead to her crown.

"Hey, Daniel, let's take a break,"
>she said as she pushed back strands of hair.

"This air is so thick you could slice it –
>it's like air you could wear!"

Gathering their hoes,
>they walked up the cucumber row

Until they came to the granite rocks
>where nothing was meant to grow.

"Daniel, look – it's a beautiful sunflower,
     with a fresh cut on the stem!"
It was laying straight upon the rocks
     like someone had placed it there for them.
"Maybe you have a secret admirer,"
     replied Daniel excitedly.
"But you know we would have heard footsteps on the rocks,
     and the only ones here are you and me."
So the girl picked up the sunflower,
     And as it reflected onto her face,
The buttery glow danced in her eyes
     As a smile she did embrace.
"I'll take it to the harvest house
     to keep it cool and out of the sun."
She placed it on a windowsill
     With questions of how this had begun.
The afternoon was scorching,
     and as she harvested crops from the back run,
She looked up to see a mother and daughter
     walking toward her at around one.
"Hello, my name is Sarah,
     and this is my daughter, Christine.
We would like to visit the garden
     and look at the vegetables you're growing."
"Do you have onions? Do you have tomatoes? Do you have cucumbers?"
     the girl questioned happily.
"I can't wait to see them growing!
     Mommy read me a garden book, you see."
"Welcome!" said the girl as the two disappeared
     into the back of the garden, towards the rear.

The vines were heavily weighted
　　　With a bountiful crop of vegetables this year
The girl bent down and continued
　　　to pull weeds as her task.
As she stood, she saw the two return:
　　　"Thank you for the visit. One question my daughter would like to ask."
"I loved looking at your vegetables – yes, each and every one!
　　　But there's something I could not find out here under the sun:
"Do you have any sunflowers?
　　　Their yellow color is so lovely!"
The girl was shocked at this request
　　　Remembering her recent sunflower discovery.
"Sadly, our sunflowers have turned brown
　　　from too much summer rain and heat –
But, come with me to the harvest house.
　　　I think you'll find something really neat!"
The sunflower glowed on the windowsill
　　　in the shadows of the afternoon sun;
Its face was turned toward the three,
　　　as it knew its work was not yet done.

The girl gently lifted the sunflower and gave it to Christine.
    "It's beautiful!" she squealed, "Just like I knew it would be!"
The girl's face beamed with rays of sunshine,
    and her heart was warm and full –
And as a single tear fell from her cheek,
    God's grace blossomed in her.
"It's like it dropped from the heavens,
    in the sun for me to find there –
For a little girl loved sunflowers,
    And I would need one to share."

"As each has received a gift, use it to serve one another, as good stewards of God's varied grace."

1 Peter 4:10 ESV

# Cat Shadows

I climb up the door,
    stand tall on the ledge;
Night skies have fallen
    on the trees and jasmine hedge.

My shadow and I
    painting on the wall,
Dark cat silhouettes,
    days approaching fall.

Ceiling cat shadows
swaying back and forth,
The door gently moves –
shadows dance some more.
"You'd better get down!
You are going to fall!"
I meow softly –
shadows on the wall.

My shadow and I
are always close by.
We will dance again
when the moon is high.

"For those who are led by the Spirit of God are the children of God."

Romans 8:14 NIV

# She Didn't Feel Like Christmas

She said that she didn't feel like Christmas,
    the spirit just wasn't there.
"Could we, please, wait to go to the market
    when I have time to spare?"

She was working quite a lot,
    rehearsals were everywhere,
Performances, musicals, parties and more;
    she had no free time to share.

One day her past violin teacher
    called to say she was in a bind.
Her accompanist for the Christmas recital
    could not help her out at this time.

So the girl agreed to accompany
    the little violinists as they played
At the Children's Memorial Hospital atrium
    on a bright, sunny Saturday.

She arrived a little bit early.
    "Mom, can I call and rant for a time?
"I'm scheduled at the bakery 'til four,
    where people are ordering 80 pies!"

"Our pies are so expensive.
    We package and bag them each day.
We take them out on a cart,
    but not one 'thank you' does the customer say!"

"The Christmas season brings out grinches
    whom your music needs to reach.
Give of your talent, be true to your heart;
    let the Lord take the lead."

All played well the Christmas songs
    we long to hear each year.
The program ended; a woman whispered,
    "You are a blessing, my dear."

The brother of a young violinist then said,
    "I play the piano too!
And one day I want to perform for little violinists,
    just like you."

She collected her Suzuki music books
    and closed the piano cover,
Just as a lady in a wheelchair asked,
    "Is the music already over?"

She gathered her coat and purse and books
and walked toward the front glass doors –
But every few steps, she turned around
and had to look at the piano once more.

"I still feel like I need to play,"
something tugged at her heart and said.
She tried to leave, looked at the piano once more –
it was like she was being lead.

The Business Office was closed, the receptionist was on the phone,
but the sign in the gift shop read, "We are always here."
"Do you think it would be okay if I played a little more?"
"As long as you like, my dear," said the lady with cheer.

People stopped by to tell her
     what a blessing she was that day.
"Did she know all the patients behind the windows
     could hear her as she played?"

A woman's nephew with open heart surgery
     was not healing as he should.
Would she play his very favorite song,
     "Over the Hill," if she could?

She played for several more hours,
     never mind that she was supposed at the bakery to be.
She answered God's calling at the hospital door
     when He tugged at her musical heart strings.

She played with joy, her heart was full;
     there was comfort and grace in the air.

Then an angel appeared who had begun this journey:
  It was the lady in the wheelchair.

The lady listened, and then she said,
  "You are a blessing, my dear.
"I was afraid that you would be gone
  before I could get back here."

The girl had played for hours,
  and it didn't seem right to end –
And when the wheelchair lady made her return,
  the message had been sent.

The girl made a hard choice to linger
and perform more music that day.
This time, there was no cash to receive –
only music from the heart to play.

But with each piece that she played,
a blessing fell from the sky.
And as she reached up to receive it,
a tear formed in her eye.

And so the girl received this gift
of fulfillment and abundant love.
Her smile was bright, her heart was full –
Christ's blessing from above.

"It is the Lord who goes before you. He will be with you; he will not leave you or forsake you. Do not fear or be dismayed."

Deuteronomy 31:8 ESV

# The Oak Tree

So, just to explain how this all came to be,
It was a cold, blustery day, around the middle of January.

I took my lunch to the table,
    Willow dish of blue and white;
Chicken soup was piping hot,
    the bow window streaming rays of light.

Suddenly, I began to feel
    the presence of another –
But, there were only my pets around me;
    there was no other.

I couldn't help but feel
     the eeriness of a stare.
I looked all around,
     seeing only the sunlight's glare.

Something told me to look "up"
     and focus on the trees,
The ones that extended beyond the roof
     and far above the leaves.

Intensely, I focused on the trunks and limbs
     of barren trees;
The oak, maple, and pecan;
     what was it I needed to see?

I remembered the "Highlights" magazines
    of childhood days gone by:
"Find the hidden picture!"
    "Oh, yes, I must try!"

There were three trees in my view:
    in the first two I saw not a thing,
But in the third tree, I saw it,
    and chimes began to sing.

Sitting high up top,
    as royal as could be,
Was an Indian face staring at me
    from up in the tall oak tree.

It was so shocking that it made me jump
    as I was sitting in my chair!
And then I spied something special
    atop the Indian's hair.

Could this be real?
    I focused hard for my eyes to clearly see.
A cross was sitting on his head,
    centered just perfectly.

"This is unbelievable," I thought.
    "I'll check for him the next day."
And there he was, yes, up in the tree,
    amid the sunlight's rays!

Now, each day we lunch together;
    I check up high in the tree.
I feel his presence as I sit,
    as we dine quietly.

It's comforting to know
    that God placed in His tree
Traces of my Indian heritage
    and the cross of Christianity.

In nature we see art,
    as art is meant to inspire.
An Indian in the tree with a cross on his head –
    I seek guidance from a Higher Power.

"But if you have been merciful, God will be merciful when He judges you."

James 2:13 NLT

# Heaven's Door

Knock, knock, knocking on Heaven's door!
What will you tell Saint Peter as entry for a tour?

Did you help the homeless child who needed food to eat?
What about the blind man who asked for help to cross the street?
Did you stop to say "thank you" to the soldier back from war?

Did you carry the elderly woman's package and ask if she had more?
Did you give to the needy what you could spare?
Did you express to your parents how much that you care?
For the mother carrying her child, did you give up your seat?
Did you spend time with the frail, the dying, and the weak?
Did you praise your child and instill confidence within?
Did you pray to your Heavenly Father again and again?
Did you toss the sidewalk musician your spare dime?
Did you spend with your family quality time?
Take time so you can truly say that you have done these things –
Then Saint Peter will surely welcome you when the doorbell rings.

And if you have ever wondered what it is like on Heaven's side,
Think on these things before you knock, and you will go through the door with pride.

Printed in the United States
By Bookmasters